CW01455990

Mercury

Despite being the smallest planet in our solar system, Mercury is the second densest planet, after Earth. This is because it has a large metallic core that makes up about 70% of its mass.

Venus

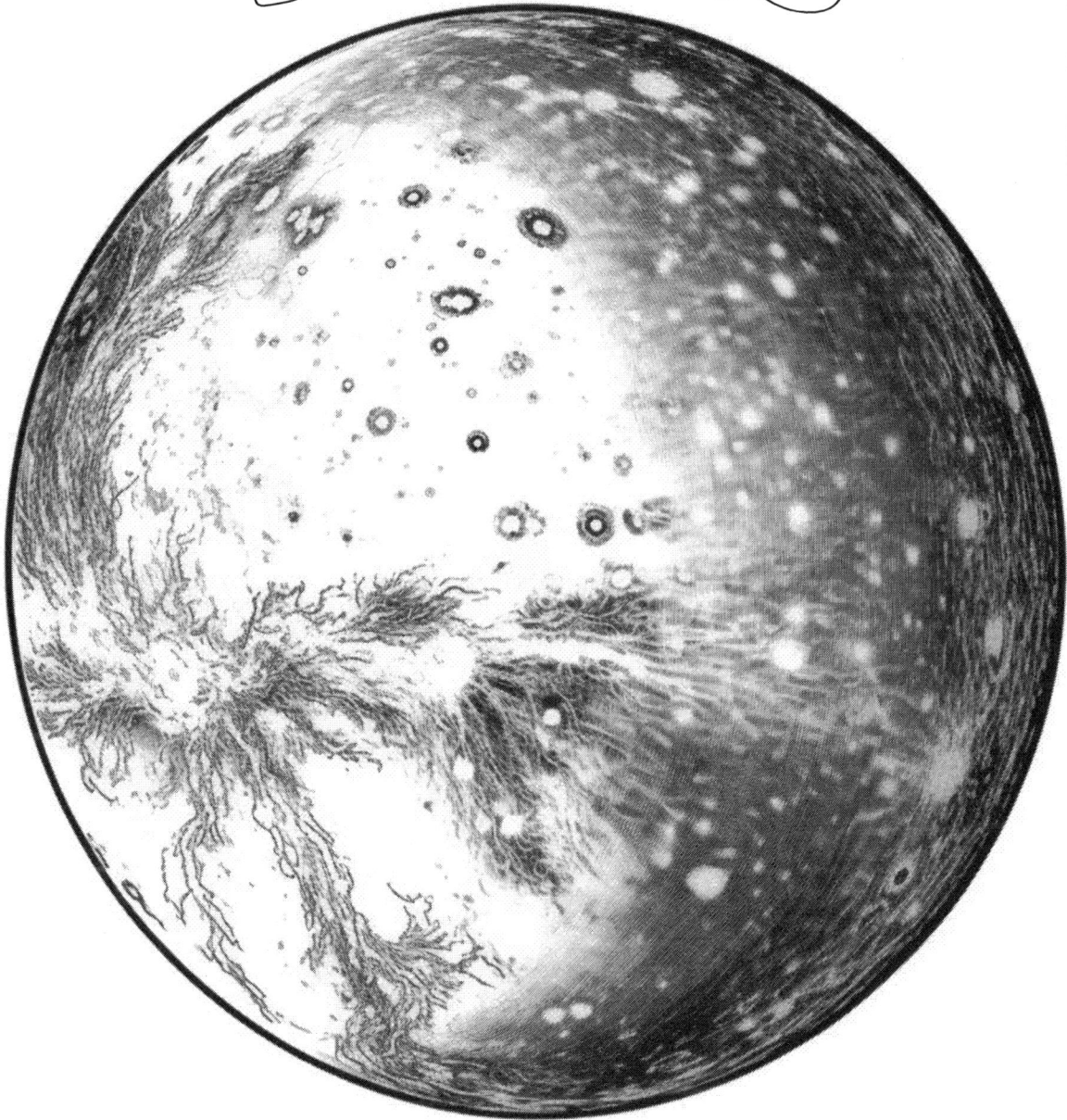

Venus rotates in the opposite direction to most other planets in our solar system, meaning that the Sun rises in the west and sets in the east on Venus. This is thought to be due to a collision with a large object early in its history, which caused it to flip its rotation.

Earth

Earth has a powerful magnetic field that is generated by its rotating, liquid iron core. This magnetic field protects the planet from the solar wind, a stream of charged particles from the Sun, which would otherwise strip away the Earth's atmosphere over time.

Mars

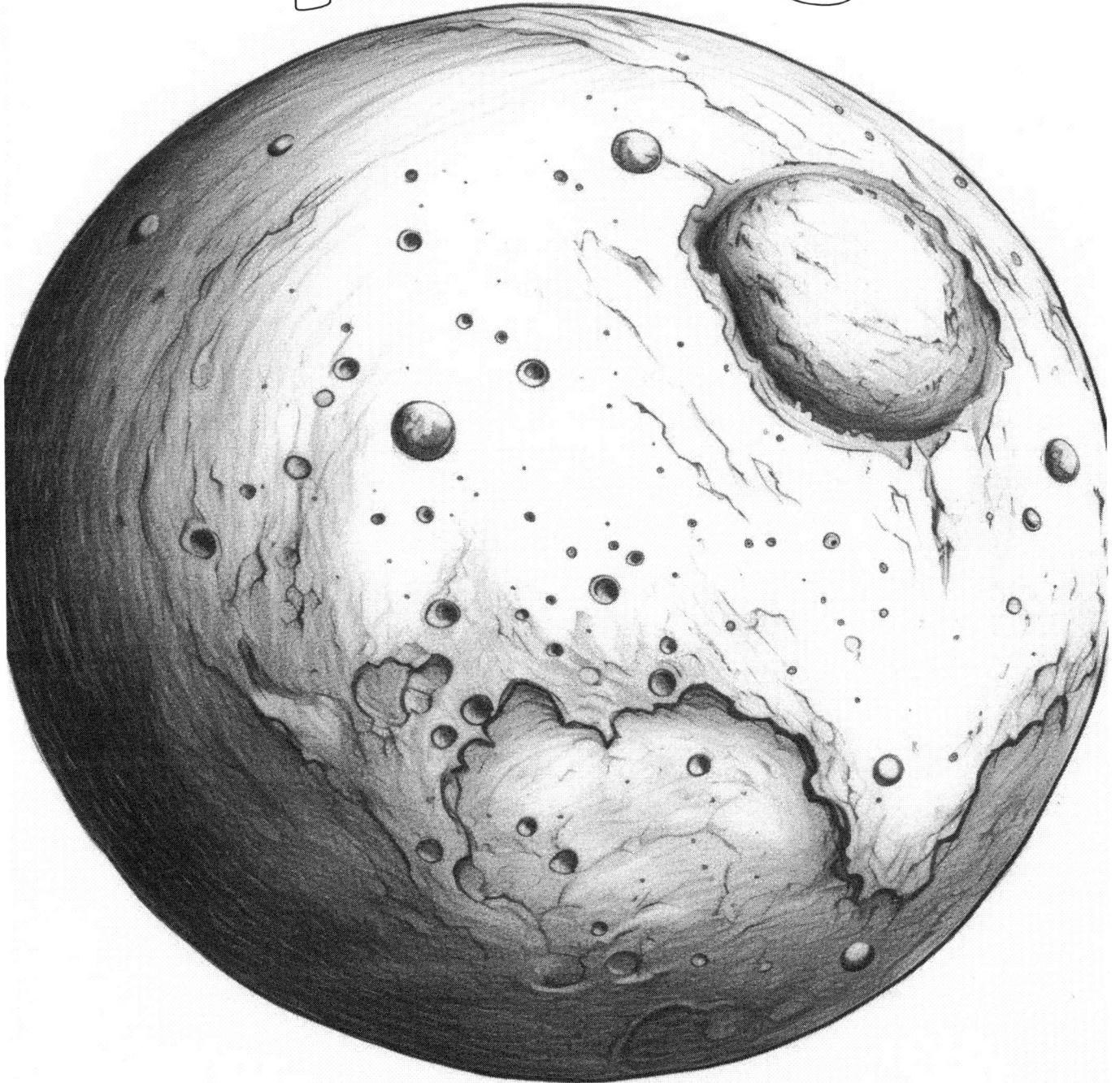

Mars is often referred to as the "Red Planet" because of its rusty-red color. This is due to the presence of iron oxide (rust) on its surface.

The asteroid belt is a region between Mars and Jupiter that contains numerous small, rocky objects (asteroids) that orbit the Sun.

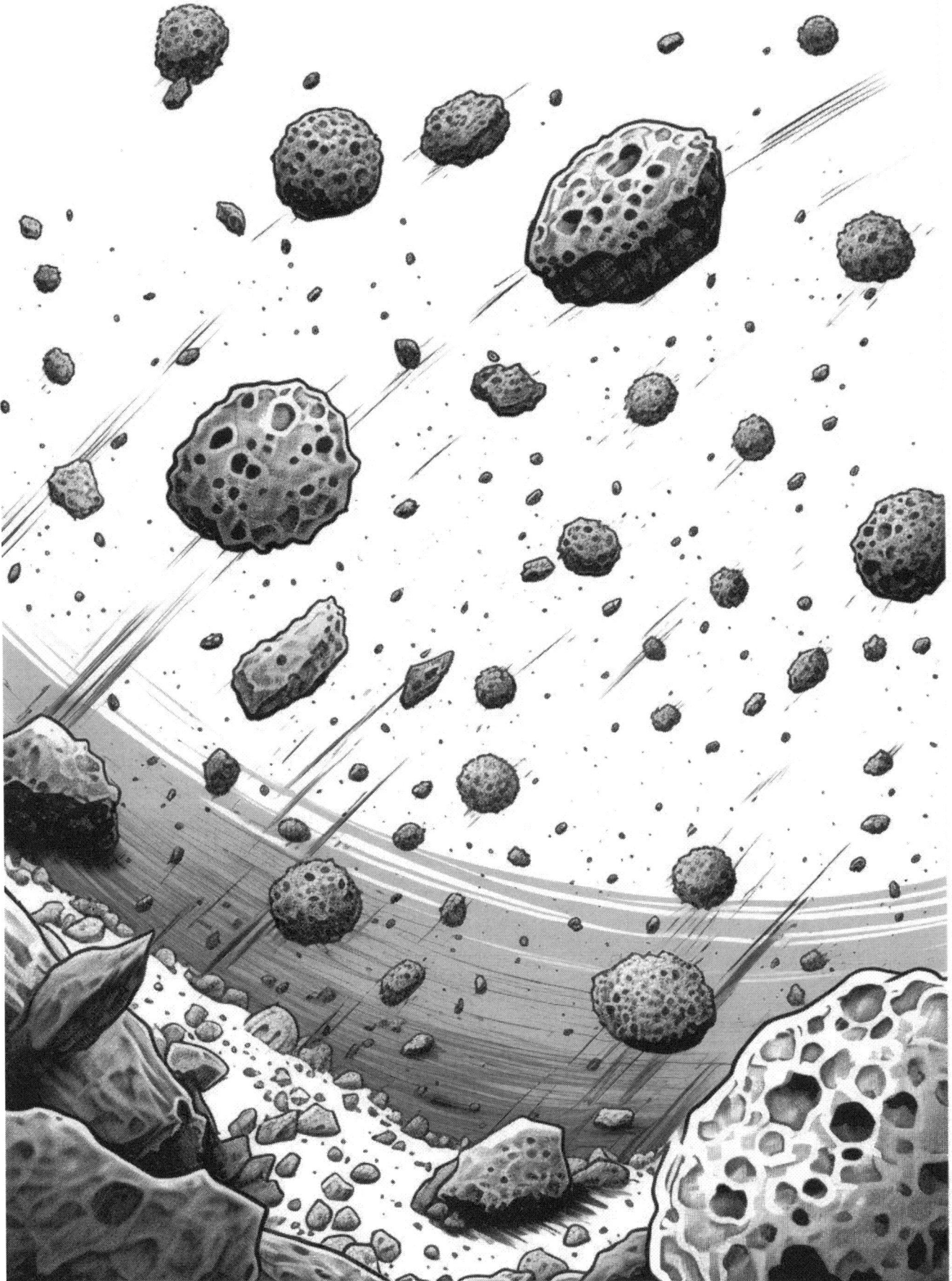

Jupiter

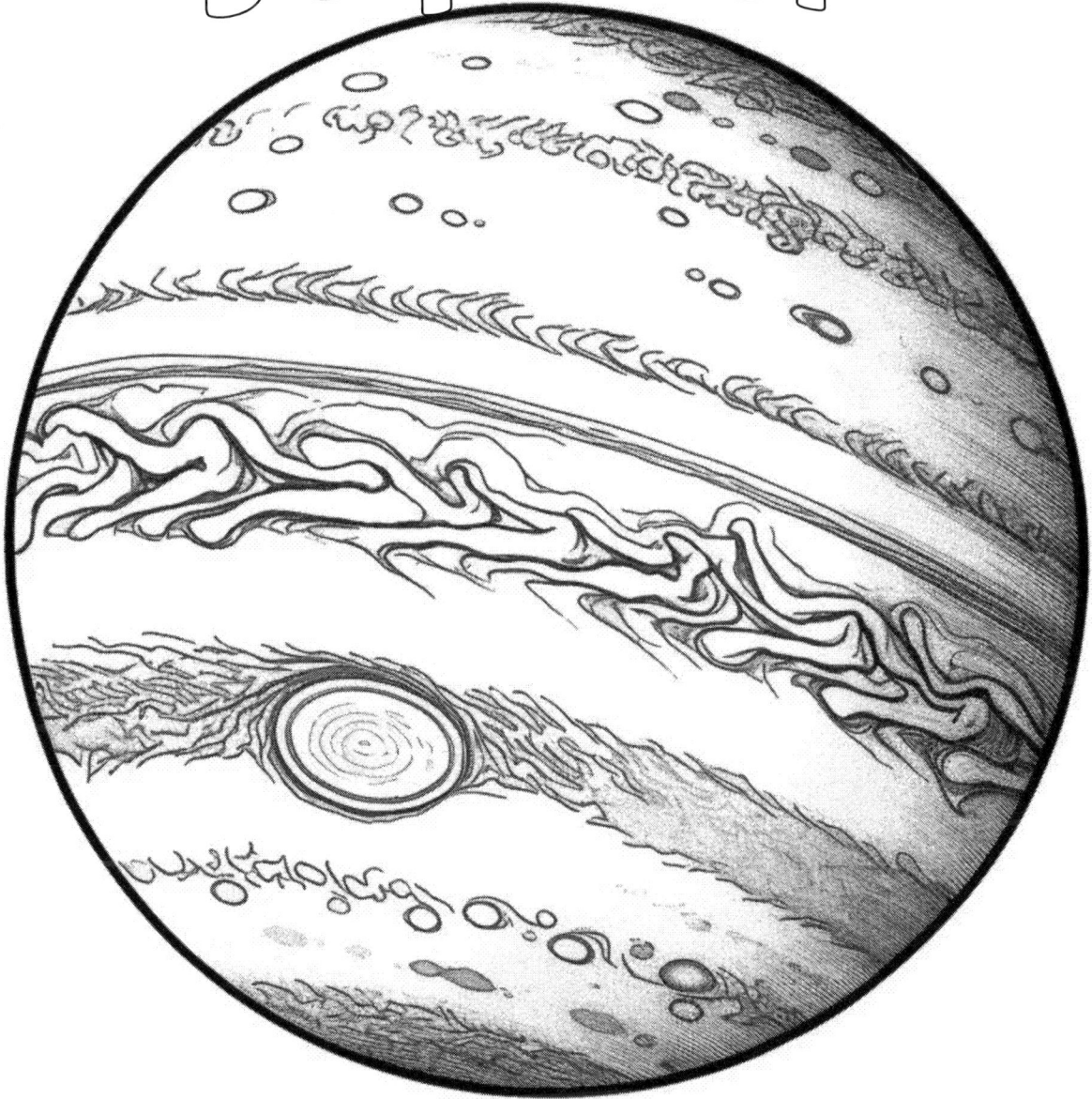

Jupiter's Great Red Spot is a giant storm on the planet's surface that is about three times the size of Earth. The storm has been raging for at least 350 years and is so large that it can be seen from Earth with a telescope.

Saturn

Saturn is known for its beautiful rings, which are made up of billions of small particles of ice and rock. The rings are relatively thin, with a thickness of about 30 feet (10 meters) but can be thousands of miles wide.

Uranus

Uranus is an ice giant, with a thick atmosphere composed mostly of hydrogen, helium, and methane. This composition gives the planet a blue-green color.

Neptune

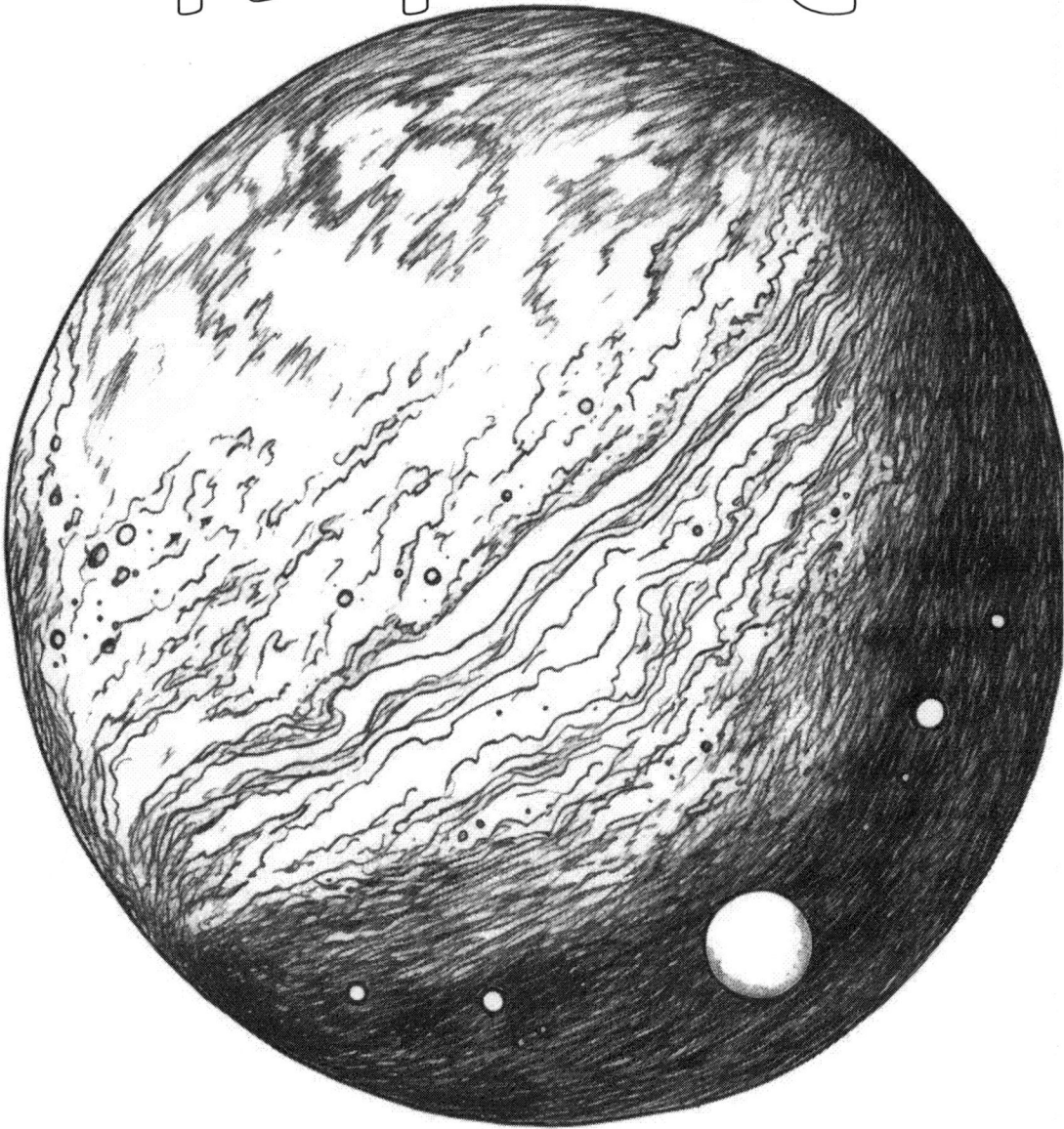

Neptune is also an ice giant and has the strongest winds of any planet in our solar system, with speeds that can exceed 1,200 miles per hour (2,000 kilometers per hour).

Pluto

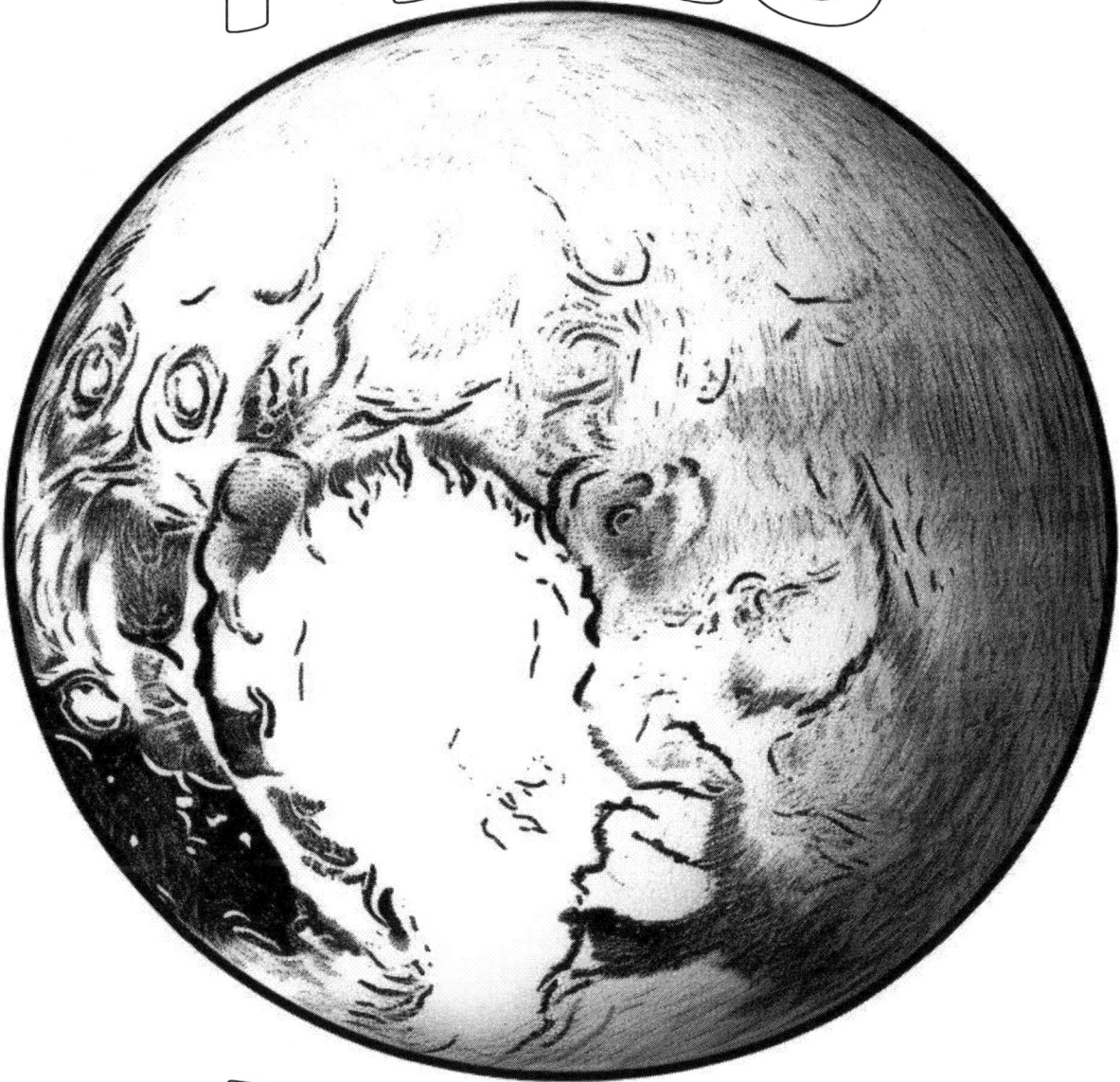

Dwarf planet

Pluto was once considered the ninth planet in our solar system and its atmosphere is believed to freeze and fall to the surface as Pluto moves away from the Sun in its orbit.

At the edge of our solar system lies the Kuiper belt, which is similar to the asteroid belt, but is far larger: 20 times as wide and 20–200 times as massive

Printed in Great Britain
by Amazon

32231479R00018